PASSIVE INCOME IDEAS AND PRACTICE FROM 2024 UPWARDS

UNLOCK YOUR FINANCIAL FREEDOM: PROVEN STRATEGIES AND PRACTICAL TIPS FOR BUILDING PASSIVE INCOME STREAMS

By

ANDREW MARK

Table Of Contents

Andrew Mark

INTRODUCTION

The pursuit of financial stability has never been more crucial especially, in an era defined by economic uncertainty and rapid technological advancement. "Passive Income Ideas & Practice" emerges as a beacon of hope, offering readers a comprehensive guide to harnessing the power of passive income streams to secure their financial future in 2024 and beyond.

This indispensable resource transcends traditional financial advice by delving into innovative strategies tailored to the contemporary landscape. Authored by a seasoned financial expert, it equips readers with the knowledge and tools necessary to navigate the complexities of passive income generation, transforming idle assets into lucrative revenue streams.

As the global economy continues to fluctuate, traditional employment models are increasingly fraught with instability. In this context, the concept of passive income emerges as a lifeline, providing individuals with a means to achieve financial independence and escape the shackles of the paycheck-to-paycheck cycle. "Passive Income Ideas & Practice" offers a roadmap for leveraging this paradigm shift, empowering readers to reclaim control over their financial destinies.

Drawing upon a diverse array of proven strategies, the book explores a multitude of passive income avenues, from real estate investments and dividend stocks to digital assets and online businesses. By presenting a comprehensive overview of these opportunities, it enables readers to identify the avenues best suited to their interests, resources, and objectives, fostering a personalized approach to wealth creation.

However, the journey to passive income is not without its challenges. The authors candidly address common pitfalls and misconceptions, illuminating the potential roadblocks that may impede progress. From initial capital constraints to the daunting prospect of market volatility, readers are armed with the knowledge needed to navigate these obstacles with confidence and resilience.

Moreover, the book emphasizes the importance of disciplined execution and strategic planning, highlighting the critical role of mindset in sustaining long-term success. By instilling readers with a proactive and forward-thinking approach, it cultivates the habits and attitudes essential for thriving in an ever-evolving economic landscape.

In addition to practical guidance, "Passive Income Ideas & Practice" provides invaluable insights gleaned from real-world experiences, featuring case studies and success stories that illustrate the transformative impact of passive income strategies. By showcasing the journeys of individuals who have achieved financial freedom through perseverance and ingenuity, it inspires readers to embark on their own path towards prosperity.

Ultimately, "Passive Income Ideas & Practice" transcends the confines of a mere financial handbook, emerging as a manifesto for empowerment and liberation. In an era marked by uncertainty and upheaval, it serves as a beacon of hope, offering a blueprint for reclaiming control over one's financial destiny and embracing a future defined by abundance and opportunity.

In an age where financial security is increasingly elusive, "Passive Income Ideas & Practice" emerges as an indispensable resource for those seeking refuge from the volatility of the modern economy. Through its pragmatic insights and unwavering optimism, it heralds a new era of financial empowerment, empowering readers to transcend the limitations of traditional employment and embark on a journey towards lasting prosperity.

CHAPTER ONE

CONCEPT OF DISCIPLINED EXECUTION, CONSISTENCY & STRATEGIC PLANNING

The concepts of disciplined execution, consistency, and strategic planning stand as pillars of success when it comes to financial independence and wealth generation, particularly in the pursuit of creating passive income streams. While the allure of passive income may evoke visions of effortless wealth, the reality often demands dedication, foresight, and a well-executed plan. Let's delve into how these principles intertwine to pave the way for sustainable passive income growth.

Disciplined Execution:

Disciplined execution involves the consistent application of predetermined strategies and actions towards a defined goal. In the context of passive income, it means adhering to investment plans, consistently allocating resources, and diligently monitoring progress. For instance, disciplined investors follow a systematic approach to asset allocation, diversification, and risk management.

Consider the case of dividend investing, a popular passive income strategy. Investors who meticulously research dividend-paying stocks, adhere to a set investment criteria, and reinvest dividends demonstrate disciplined execution. Over time, this approach can yield substantial returns, as evidenced by historical data showing the compounding power of reinvested dividends.

Consistency:

Consistency complements disciplined execution by reinforcing habits and routines conducive to passive income generation. Consistency involves staying committed to long-term objectives despite market fluctuations or temporary setbacks. It entails regular contributions, whether financial or effort-based, towards income-producing assets.

Real estate investing exemplifies the significance of consistency. Property owners who consistently maintain their assets, diligently screen tenants, and reinvest rental income into property improvements foster sustainable income streams. Over time, the compounding effects of rental cash flow and property appreciation amplify wealth accumulation.

Strategic Planning:

Strategic planning provides the roadmap for achieving passive income goals by aligning resources with opportunities and risk management strategies. It involves analyzing market trends, identifying income-generating assets, and formulating a cohesive plan tailored to individual circumstances and objectives.

The growth of passive income through online businesses illustrates the importance of strategic planning. Entrepreneurs who conduct market research, develop scalable business models, and implement effective marketing strategies position themselves for long-term success. By leveraging automation and outsourcing, they create systems that generate income with minimal ongoing effort.

Statistics:

Statistics underscore the efficacy of disciplined execution, consistency, and strategic planning in passive income endeavors. According to a study by Vanguard, disciplined investors who adhered to a long-term investment strategy outperformed those who attempted to time the market. Similarly, research by the National Association of Realtors highlights the steady appreciation of real estate values over time, emphasizing the benefits of consistent property ownership.

Summarily, in the pursuit of creating passive income streams, disciplined execution, consistency, and strategic planning emerge as indispensable tools for success. Whether through dividend investing, real estate ownership, or online entrepreneurship, adhering to these principles lays the foundation for sustainable wealth accumulation. By embracing a proactive mindset and staying committed to long-term objectives, individuals can navigate the complexities of financial markets and realize their aspirations of financial independence.

CHAPTER TWO

COMMON PITFALLS AND MISCONCEPTIONS ABOUT PASSIVE INCOME

Passive income: the dream of earning money while you sleep, a concept that has captured the imagination of many aspiring entrepreneurs and investors. Yet, behind the allure lies a landscape fraught with pitfalls and misconceptions that can derail even the most well-intentioned efforts. To succeed in creating a sustainable passive income stream, one must first recognize and navigate these obstacles.

Misconception 1: Passive Income Requires No Effort

One of the most pervasive myths surrounding passive income is that it requires no effort once set up. While it's true that passive income streams can generate revenue with minimal day-to-day involvement, achieving this level of automation often demands significant upfront work. For instance, creating an eBook or an online course requires extensive planning, content creation, and marketing efforts before it can generate consistent income without continuous input.

Misconception 2: Passive Income is Always Passive

Another common pitfall is the belief that passive income is entirely hands-off. In reality, passive income streams often require ongoing maintenance and optimization to remain profitable. Real estate investments, for example, demand periodic property management, tenant communication, and upkeep to preserve their value and generate returns.

Misconception 3: Passive Income Guarantees Financial Freedom

While passive income can be a powerful tool for building wealth, it's not a guaranteed path to financial freedom. Many factors, including market fluctuations, economic downturns, and unforeseen expenses, can impact the stability and profitability of passive income streams. Over-reliance on a single source of passive income without diversification can expose individuals to significant financial risks.

Misconception 4: Passive Income is Quick and Easy

The allure of quick and effortless riches often leads individuals to fall prey to get-rich-quick schemes promising overnight success. However, legitimate passive income streams typically require time, patience, and persistence to build. For instance, affiliate marketing or blogging may take months or even years to gain traction and generate substantial income.

To illustrate the importance of dispelling these misconceptions, consider the example of affiliate marketing. While it's touted as a passive income opportunity, success in affiliate marketing hinges on creating valuable content, building an engaged audience, and continuously refining marketing strategies. According to a study by VigLink, only 9% of affiliates drive 58% of revenue, highlighting the disparity in outcomes and the necessity of ongoing effort.

Moreover, diversification is key to mitigating risks associated with passive income endeavors. Investors who rely solely on one income stream, such as rental properties, may face significant challenges during economic downturns or shifts in market conditions. By diversifying across multiple assets classes, industries, or revenue streams, individuals can safeguard their financial interests and enhance long-term sustainability.

In conclusion, while the promise of passive income is enticing, it's essential to approach it with a clear understanding of the challenges and realities involved. By dispelling common misconceptions and avoiding pitfalls such as unrealistic expectations, lack of diversification, and passive involvement, aspiring entrepreneurs can increase their likelihood of success in creating sustainable passive income streams. Ultimately, patience, perseverance, and prudent decision-making are indispensable qualities on the journey to financial independence through passive income.

CHAPTER THREE

INVESTMENT INCOME

Investment income stands as a stalwart among passive income streams, offering financial stability and growth potential. Through strategic allocation of funds into assets such as stocks, bonds, and real estate, investors can generate consistent returns without active involvement. Dividends from stocks, interest from bonds, and rental income from real estate are examples of investment income sources. By diligently managing portfolios and staying informed about market trends, individuals can cultivate a reliable stream of passive income, enhancing financial security and paving the way for long-term wealth accumulation.

The following are examples of investment income ideas:

Dividend Stocks

Bonds

Mutual Funds/ETFs

Real Estate Investment Trusts (REITs)

Peer-to-Peer Lending

Crowd-funding Investments

DIVIDEND STOCKS

Dividends are a form of passive income generated from owning shares of publicly traded companies. When companies earn profits, they may choose to distribute a portion of those profits to shareholders in the form of dividends. This income stream allows investors to benefit from the success of the companies they invest in without actively participating in their operations.

Dividends can provide a steady stream of income, often paid out quarterly, making them an attractive option for individuals seeking to supplement their earnings or build long-term wealth. Additionally, dividends can offer a hedge against inflation and market volatility, as well as potential tax advantages depending on the investor's tax bracket and jurisdiction.

PROFITABILITY

The profitability of dividends as a passive income source depends on several factors, including the dividend yield of the stocks in which you invest, the stability and growth potential of the underlying companies, and the size of your investment portfolio.

Dividend yields vary among companies and industries, with some offering higher yields than others. Generally, established companies with strong cash flows and a history of consistent dividend payments tend to offer more reliable income streams. However, higher yields may also come with higher risks, such as companies facing financial difficulties or uncertain market conditions.

Over time, reinvesting dividends and compounding returns can significantly enhance the profitability of this passive income strategy. By reinvesting dividends to purchase additional shares, investors can benefit from the power of compounding, allowing their investment to grow exponentially over the long term.

START-UP COST AND EQUIPMENT

The startup cost for investing in dividend-paying stocks can vary depending on individual preferences and financial circumstances. In general, investors can start with as little or as much capital as they are comfortable with, making dividends accessible to a wide range of investors.

To begin investing in dividends, you'll need:

1. *Capital*: The amount of money you're willing to invest in dividend-paying stocks.

2. *Brokerage Account*: A brokerage account allows you to buy and sell stocks on the stock market. Choose a reputable brokerage platform that offers competitive fees and a user-friendly interface.

3. *Research Tools*: Utilize research tools and resources to evaluate potential dividend-paying stocks. Look for companies with a history of consistent dividend payments, strong financial performance, and growth prospects.

4. ***Diversification Strategy***: Consider diversifying your investment portfolio across different sectors and industries to mitigate risk and maximize returns.

HOW TO DO IT

1. Research and Select Dividend-Paying Stocks: Conduct thorough research to identify companies with a track record of consistent dividend payments, strong financial health, and growth potential. Look for companies with sustainable dividend yields and a history of increasing dividends over time.

2. Open a Brokerage Account: Choose a reputable brokerage platform and open an account. Ensure the platform offers access to a wide range of dividend-paying stocks and provides the tools and resources you need to make informed investment decisions.

3. Allocate Capital: Determine how much capital you're willing to invest in dividend-paying stocks. Consider your financial goals, risk tolerance, and investment time horizon when allocating capital to your dividend portfolio.

4. Monitor and Reinvest Dividends: Monitor the performance of your dividend-paying stocks regularly and reinvest dividends to purchase additional shares. Reinvesting dividends allows you to leverage the power of compounding, accelerating the growth of your investment portfolio over time.

5. Stay Informed and Adjust: Stay informed about market trends, company news, and economic developments that may impact your dividend investments. Be prepared to adjust your investment strategy as needed to adapt to changing market conditions and achieve your financial goals.

By following these steps and remaining disciplined in your investment approach, you can build a diversified portfolio of dividend-paying stocks that generate a reliable stream of passive income and contribute to your long-term financial success. Remember to seek guidance from financial professionals if needed and stay committed to your investment strategy over the long term.

BONDS

Bonds are a form of fixed-income investment where investors lend money to entities such as corporations or governments in exchange for periodic interest payments and the return of the principal amount at maturity. Bonds are considered a relatively stable investment compared to stocks, making them a popular choice for passive income seekers looking for steady returns.

PROFITABILITY

Profitability in bonds primarily comes from the interest payments, also known as coupon payments, received over the bond's lifespan. The profitability of bonds can vary depending on factors such as the bond's coupon rate, maturity date, and prevailing interest rates. Typically, higher coupon rates or longer maturity periods offer higher returns but may also come with higher risks.

As of 2024, estimated yields on bonds can range from 2% to 6%, depending on the type of bonds and prevailing market conditions. For example, government bonds tend to offer lower yields but are considered safer, while corporate bonds may offer higher yields but come with higher risk.

STARTUP COST AND EQUIPMENT

The startup cost for investing in bonds can vary depending on the type of bonds you choose and the minimum investment requirements set by brokers or financial institutions. Generally, the initial investment for bonds can range from a few hundred to several thousand dollars.

Equipment needed for investing in bonds is minimal and typically involves:

1. Computer or Smartphone: You'll need a device with internet access to research and monitor bond investments.

2. *Brokerage Account*: Open an account with a brokerage firm or financial institution that offers bond trading services. Many online brokerages provide access to a wide range of bond offerings.

3. *Capital*: Allocate funds for purchasing bonds based on your investment goals and risk tolerance.

HOW TO DO IT

1. Research and Education: Start by learning about the different types of bonds available, such as government bonds, municipal bonds, corporate bonds, and treasury bonds. Understand how bonds work, including key concepts like coupon rates, maturity dates, and credit ratings.

2. Determine Investment Goals and Risk Tolerance: Assess your investment objectives, whether it's generating passive income, preserving capital, or diversifying your investment portfolio. Consider your risk tolerance and investment time-frame when selecting bonds.

3. Select Bonds: Research and analyze available bonds to identify suitable investment opportunities. Look for bonds with strong credit ratings, attractive coupon rates, and suitable maturity periods. Diversify your bond portfolio to spread risk across different issuers and sectors.

4. Purchase Bonds: Once you've identified suitable bonds, place buy orders through your brokerage account. Pay attention to transaction costs and fees associated with bond purchases. Consider using limit orders to ensure you get a favorable price.

5. Monitor and Rebalance: Regularly monitor your bond investments to track performance, assess changes in interest rates, and evaluate credit risks. Rebalance your bond portfolio as needed to maintain your desired asset allocation and risk profile.

Example:

Let's say you have $10,000 to invest in bonds. After researching various options, you decide to allocate your investment as follows:

- $5,000 in government bonds with a 5% coupon rate and a 10-year maturity.

- $3,000 in investment-grade corporate bonds with a 4% coupon rate and a 5-year maturity.

- $2,000 in municipal bonds with a 3% coupon rate and a 7-year maturity.

Over the investment period, you would receive regular coupon payments from each bond, providing you with a stream of passive income. At maturity, you would also receive the principal amount back for each bond, assuming no default or early redemption.

By following these steps and managing your bond investments effectively, you can generate passive income and build wealth over time through bond investments. However, it's essential to conduct thorough research, diversify your investments, and stay informed about market developments to make informed investment decisions.

MUTUAL FUNDS/ETFs

Investing in Mutual Funds and Exchange-Traded Funds (ETFs) is a popular strategy for generating passive income. These investment vehicles pool money from multiple investors to invest in diversified portfolios of stocks, bonds, or other assets. Unlike actively managed funds, mutual funds and ETFs typically follow a passive investment strategy, aiming to match the performance of a specific index.

PROFITABILITY

The profitability of investing in mutual funds and ETFs varies depending on factors such as the performance of the underlying assets, management fees, and market conditions. On average, mutual funds and ETFs can generate returns ranging from 5% to 10% annually, although this can fluctuate significantly over time.

For example, if you invest $10,000 in an ETF with an average annual return of 7%, you could potentially earn around $700 in passive income per year. Over the long term, compounding returns can significantly increase your wealth.

STARTUP COST AND EQUIPMENT

The startup cost for investing in mutual funds and ETFs can be relatively low compared to other investment opportunities. You'll need a brokerage account to buy and sell mutual funds and ETFs, which may require an initial deposit ranging from $0 to $1,000, depending on the platform.

Additionally, you may incur fees associated with buying and selling funds, as well as annual management fees charged by the fund provider. These fees typically range from 0.05% to 2% of your total investment annually.

HOW TO DO IT

1. Research and Select Funds: Start by researching different mutual funds and ETFs to identify ones that align with your investment goals, risk tolerance, and time horizon. Look for funds with low expense ratios and strong historical performance.

2. *Open a Brokerage Account*: Choose a reputable brokerage platform that offers access to a wide range of mutual funds and ETFs. Popular options include Vanguard, Fidelity, and Charles Schwab. Follow the account opening process, which typically involves providing personal information and funding your account.

3. *Diversify Your Portfolio*: Invest in a diversified portfolio of mutual funds and ETFs to spread risk and maximize potential returns. Consider allocating your investments across different asset classes, sectors, and geographic regions to minimize volatility.

4. *Regularly Monitor and Rebalance*: Keep track of your investments and periodically review your portfolio to ensure it remains aligned with your financial goals.

Rebalance your portfolio as needed to maintain your desired asset allocation and risk level.

5. **Reinvest Dividends**: Many mutual funds and ETFs pay dividends regularly, which can be reinvested to purchase additional shares and compound your returns over time. Reinvesting dividends can accelerate wealth accumulation and boost your passive income stream.

6. **Stay Informed and Educated**: Stay informed about market developments, economic trends, and changes in fund performance. Continuously educate yourself about investing principles and strategies to make informed decisions and adapt to evolving market conditions.

Example:

Let's say you decide to invest in a diversified ETF such as the Vanguard Total Stock Market ETF (VTI). You open a brokerage account with Vanguard and invest

$10,000 in VTI, which has an expense ratio of 0.03% per year. Assuming an average annual return of 7%, your investment could potentially generate around $700 in passive income annually, excluding any dividends reinvested. Over time, as your investment grows and compounds, your passive income stream could increase significantly, providing financial stability and long-term wealth accumulation.

REAL ESTATE INVESTMENT TRUSTS (REITS)

Real Estate Investment Trusts (REITs) provide a unique opportunity for individuals to invest in real estate without directly owning or managing properties. REITs are companies that own, operate, or finance income-generating real estate across various sectors, including residential, commercial, and industrial properties.

Investors can buy shares of REITs, which trade on major stock exchanges, allowing them to earn dividends from rental income, property sales, and mortgage interest. This investment vehicle offers diversification, liquidity, and the potential for passive income, making it an attractive option for those seeking to build wealth through real estate.

PROFITABILITY

The profitability of investing in REITs can vary depending on factors such as market conditions, property performance, and dividend yields. Historically, REITs have delivered competitive returns, with average annual total returns ranging from 8% to 12%. Additionally, REITs typically distribute at least 90% of their taxable income to shareholders in the form of dividends, providing investors with a steady stream of passive income. Dividend yields for REITs commonly range from 3% to 6%, offering an attractive alternative to traditional fixed-income investments like bonds.

STARTUP COST AND EQUIPMENT

The startup cost for investing in REITs is relatively low compared to purchasing physical properties. Investors can start with as little as a few hundred dollars to purchase shares of publicly traded REITs through a brokerage account. While there are no specific equipment requirements for investing in REITs, investors will need access to a computer or smartphone to research and trade REIT shares online. Depending on the brokerage platform chosen, investors may also incur trading commissions, which typically range from $0 to $10 per trade.

HOW TO DO IT

Investing in REITs is straightforward and accessible to both novice and experienced investors. Here's a step-by-step guide on how to get started:

1. Research and Select REITs: Conduct thorough research to identify REITs that align with your investment goals, risk tolerance, and preferred property sectors. Consider factors such as dividend yield, historical performance, property holdings, and management track record. Realistic Example: Suppose you're interested in diversifying your portfolio with a mix of residential and commercial properties. You research and identify several REITs with strong track records in these sectors, such as Equity Residential (residential) and Simon Property Group (commercial).

2. Open a Brokerage Account: Choose a reputable brokerage platform that offers access to a wide range of REITs and provides competitive trading fees. Complete the account opening process, which typically involves providing personal information, funding your account, and agreeing to terms and conditions.

3. Purchase REIT Shares: Once your brokerage account is set up and funded, you can start investing in REITs by placing buy orders for shares through the brokerage platform. Specify the quantity of shares you wish to purchase and review the current market price before placing your order.

4. Monitor and Rebalance: Regularly monitor the performance of your REIT investments and make adjustments to your portfolio as needed. Reinvest dividends to compound your returns over time and consider rebalancing your portfolio to maintain diversification and align with your investment objectives.

5. *Stay Informed*: Stay informed about market trends, economic indicators, and regulatory developments that may impact the performance of REITs. Utilize resources such as financial news websites, investment publications, and company reports to stay updated on relevant information.

By following these steps and staying informed about market dynamics, investors can effectively build wealth and generate passive income through investments in Real Estate Investment Trusts (REITs). With relatively low startup costs, accessibility, and the potential for attractive returns, REITs offer a compelling opportunity for individuals looking to diversify their investment portfolios and achieve long-term financial goals.

PEER TO PEER LENDING

Peer-to-peer lending, also known as P2P lending, is a form of lending that connects borrowers with individual lenders through online platforms, bypassing traditional financial institutions like banks. It allows individuals to lend money directly to others in exchange for interest payments, providing an alternative investment opportunity for lenders and access to funding for borrowers.

PROFITABILITY

Profitability in peer-to-peer lending can vary depending on several factors, including the platform used, the risk level of loans, and market conditions. On average, lenders can expect to earn annual returns ranging from 4% to 7%, although some platforms may offer higher returns for riskier loans. For example, on a $10,000 investment, a 6% return would yield $600 in annual interest income.

STARTUP COST AND EQUIPMENT

The startup costs for peer-to-peer lending are relatively low compared to other investment opportunities. Typically, all you need is a computer or smartphone with internet access to register on a P2P lending platform and start lending. Some platforms may require a minimum initial investment, which can range from $25 to $1,000 or more depending on the platform and the individual's preferences.

HOW TO DO IT

1. Research P2P Lending Platforms: Begin by researching and comparing different P2P lending platforms to find one that aligns with your investment goals and risk tolerance. Examples of popular platforms include LendingClub, Prosper, and Funding Circle.

2. *Create an Account*: Once you've chosen a platform, create an account and complete the necessary verification steps, which may include providing personal information and linking a bank account for funds transfer.

3. *Diversify Your Investments*: Spread your investment across multiple loans to minimize risk. Most platforms offer automated investment tools that allow you to diversify your portfolio by automatically allocating funds to a variety of loans based on your specified criteria.

4. *Monitor and Manage Your Investments*: Keep track of your investments and monitor borrower repayment performance. Some platforms provide tools and dashboards to help you track your portfolio's performance and make informed decisions about reinvesting or withdrawing funds.

5. *Reinvest Returns*: As you earn interest income from your investments, consider reinvesting those returns to compound your earnings over time. Reinvesting can accelerate wealth accumulation and help you achieve your financial goals faster.

Example: Gabriel decides to start peer-to-peer lending with an initial investment of $1,000 on LendingClub. He diversifies his investment by spreading it across 40 different loans, each with an average loan size of $25. Over the course of a year, he earns an average return of 6%, generating $60 in interest income. Gabriel decides to reinvest his returns to further grow his portfolio and increase his passive income over time.

Peer-to-peer lending offers individuals an opportunity to earn passive income by lending money to borrowers through online platforms. With low startup costs and the potential for attractive returns, it can be a viable addition to an investment portfolio. However, it's essential to conduct thorough research, diversify investments, and monitor performance to maximize returns and manage risk effectively.

CROWD-FUNDING INVESTMENTS

Crowd-funding investment involves pooling money from a large number of individuals to invest in various projects, businesses, or ventures. This method allows investors to collectively support initiatives they believe in while potentially earning returns on their investments. Crowd-funding platforms serve as intermediaries, connecting investors with entrepreneurs or project creators seeking funding.

PROFITABILITY:

The profitability of crowd-funding investment can vary widely depending on the projects or ventures funded. Returns may range from modest to substantial, and there's also the risk of losing some or all of the invested capital. Prize estimates are difficult to provide as they depend on the success of individual projects and the specific terms of investment agreements. However, some successful crowd-funding projects have generated significant returns for investors, sometimes surpassing traditional investment vehicles.

STARTUP COST AND EQUIPMENT:

Startup costs for crowd-funding investment are relatively low compared to other investment avenues. Typically, investors need a computer or smartphone with internet access to browse and invest through crowd-funding platforms. Many platforms have no minimum investment requirements, allowing investors to start with small amounts. However, it's essential to factor in potential investment losses and platform fees when budgeting for crowd-funding investments.

HOW TO DO IT:

1. Choose a Crowd-funding Platform: Research and select a reputable crowd-funding platform that aligns with your investment goals and risk tolerance. Examples include Kickstarter, Indiegogo, SeedInvest, and Patreon.

2. Browse Projects: Explore the projects listed on the chosen platform and conduct thorough due diligence. Evaluate factors such as the project's business model, team expertise, market potential, and investment terms.

3. Invest Wisely: Once you've identified promising projects, consider diversifying your investments across multiple ventures to spread risk. Carefully review the investment terms, including the expected returns, timeframe, and any associated risks or restrictions.

4. Monitor Investments: Stay engaged with your investments by monitoring project updates, financial performance, and any relevant communications from project creators. Some crowdfunding platforms provide regular updates to investors on the progress of funded projects.

5. Manage Risks: Understand that investing in crowdfunding carries inherent risks, including the potential loss of capital. Be prepared to accept the possibility of investment losses and avoid investing more than you can afford to lose.

6. ***Reinvest Profits***: If your investments generate returns, consider reinvesting profits into new projects or diversifying your portfolio further to maximize long-term growth potential.

Example:

Luke, an investor interested in supporting innovative startups, decides to explore crowdfunding investment opportunities. After researching various crowdfunding platforms, he chooses SeedInvest for its focus on early-stage companies. Luke browses through the platform's listings and identifies a tech startup developing a groundbreaking medical device. Impressed by the project's potential and the experienced team behind it, Luke decides to invest $1,000 in exchange for equity.

Over the following years, the startup successfully launches its product, attracts additional funding, and eventually gets acquired by a larger healthcare corporation. As a result, Luke's initial $1,000 investment grows substantially, providing him with a significant return on investment.

This example illustrates how crowd-funding investment can offer opportunities for individuals to support innovative ventures while potentially earning returns on their investments. However, it's crucial to conduct thorough research, manage risks effectively, and diversify investments to enhance the likelihood of success.

CHAPTER FOUR

RENTAL INCOME

Rental income offers a lucrative avenue for passive earnings. By leasing out property, whether residential or commercial, landlords generate consistent revenue streams. This income can offset mortgage payments, provide financial stability, and even yield profits. However, successful rental income requires careful property management, tenant selection, and adherence to local regulations. Despite challenges, rental income remains a popular investment strategy due to its potential for long-term financial growth and diversification.

REAL ESTATE RENTALS

Investing in real estate rentals offers a lucrative opportunity to generate passive income streams while building long-term wealth. By purchasing properties and renting them out to tenants, individuals can capitalize on the growing demand for housing while diversifying their investment portfolio.

STARTUP COST:

The startup costs for real estate rentals vary depending on factors such as location, property type, and market conditions. On average, investors should budget for expenses such as down payments (typically 20% of the property's purchase price), closing costs, property maintenance, insurance, and any necessary renovations or repairs.

In the United States, for example, the median home price is around $300,000. With a 20% down payment, investors would need approximately $60,000 upfront, excluding additional expenses. However, real estate markets vary globally, and start-up costs can range significantly based on regional factors.

PROFITABILITY:

Real estate rentals can be highly profitable ventures, offering both ongoing rental income and potential appreciation in property value over time. The profitability of rental properties depends on factors such as rental rates, occupancy rates, property appreciation, and operating expenses.

As an illustration, consider a rental property with a monthly rental income of $1,500 and annual operating expenses of $8,000 (including property taxes, insurance, maintenance, and vacancy costs). With an annual rental income of $18,000 ($1,500 x 12 months) and operating expenses of $8,000, the property's net operating income (NOI) would be $10,000.

To determine profitability, investors can calculate key financial metrics such as the capitalization rate (cap rate) and cash-on-cash return. These metrics assess the return on investment relative to the property's purchase price and the investor's initial cash outlay.

HOW TO DO IT:

1. Research and Analysis: Start by researching real estate markets to identify areas with strong rental demand, favorable economic indicators, and potential for property appreciation. Analyze rental rates, vacancy rates, and comparable property sales to assess investment opportunities.

2. Secure Financing: Determine the financing option that best suits your investment strategy, whether it's conventional mortgages, FHA loans, or private financing.

Obtain pre-approval from lenders to strengthen your negotiating position and streamline the purchase process.

3. *Property Selection*: Choose properties that align with your investment goals and budget constraints. Consider factors such as location, property condition, rental potential, and projected cash flow. Conduct thorough inspections and due diligence to assess the property's condition and potential risks.

4. *Tenant Screening*: Implement rigorous tenant screening processes to mitigate the risk of rental defaults and property damage. Verify prospective tenants' income, employment history, creditworthiness, and rental references to ensure they meet your criteria.

5. *Property Management*: Decide whether to manage the property yourself or enlist the services of a professional property management company. Property managers can handle tasks such as rent collection, maintenance, tenant communication, and lease enforcement, allowing investors to focus on other aspects of their investment portfolio.

6. *Continuous Monitoring and Optimization*: Regularly monitor your rental properties' performance and make adjustments as needed to maximize profitability. Stay informed about market trends, rental demand, and regulatory changes that may impact your investment strategy. Consider implementing strategies such as rent increases, property upgrades, or refinancing to optimize cash flow and enhance long-term returns.

By following these steps and leveraging available resources, aspiring real estate investors can embark on their journey to building a successful rental property portfolio. With careful planning, diligent execution, and a long-term perspective, real estate rentals can serve as a valuable vehicle for wealth creation and financial independence.

EQUIPMENT RENTALS

Equipment rentals offer a practical solution for individuals and businesses needing access to specialized tools or machinery without the burden of ownership. Whether it's construction equipment, party supplies, or household appliances, renting provides flexibility and cost-effectiveness. This business model capitalizes on the sharing economy trend, where assets are utilized more efficiently, benefiting both providers and renters.

START-UP COST: The start-up costs for an equipment rental business can vary depending on the scale and scope of operations. Here's a breakdown of potential expenses:

*1. **Inventory:*** Acquiring a diverse range of equipment will be your primary investment. Costs can range from a few thousand dollars for small tools and appliances to several hundred thousand for heavy machinery like excavators or forklifts.

*2. **Storage Facility***: Renting or purchasing a warehouse or storage space to store and maintain your equipment is essential. Prices vary based on location and size but could range from $1,000 to $5,000 per month.

*3. **Insurance***: Liability insurance to protect against damages or accidents involving rented equipment is crucial. Costs can vary widely based on coverage and the value of your inventory but may start around $1,000 annually.

4. Transportation: Factor in expenses for transporting equipment to and from rental locations. This includes vehicle maintenance, fuel, and possibly hiring drivers or renting trucks.

5. Marketing and Operations: Budget for marketing efforts to attract customers, as well as administrative expenses like website development, software for inventory management, and staffing.

Overall, start-up costs can range from $50,000 to $500,000 or more, depending on the size and scope of your rental operation.

PROFITABILITY

The profitability of an equipment rental business can be lucrative, with the potential for high margins. Let's consider a hypothetical scenario:

Assuming you have invested $200,000 in inventory and operational expenses, and your average monthly revenue is $30,000. After deducting operating costs (including insurance, maintenance, and marketing) of $15,000 per month, your monthly profit would be $15,000.

With careful management and scaling of your business, annual profits could range from $100,000 to $500,000 or more, depending on market demand and competition.

HOW TO DO IT

1. Identify Niche Markets: Research local demand and competition to identify underserved niche markets. For example, catering to the film industry with specialized camera equipment or targeting DIY homeowners with tool rentals for home improvement projects.

2. Offer Convenient Rental Terms: Provide flexible rental periods, competitive pricing, and convenient pickup/delivery options to attract customers. Consider offering discounts for long-term rentals or package deals for multiple items.

3. Invest in Quality Equipment: Ensure your inventory consists of well-maintained, high-quality equipment to build trust with customers and minimize downtime due to repairs.

4. Market Strategically: Utilize online platforms, social media, and partnerships with local businesses to promote your rental services. Target advertising towards specific industries or events where your equipment would be in high demand.

5. Provide Excellent Customer Service: Offer knowledgeable staff who can assist customers in selecting the right equipment for their needs and provide guidance on proper usage and safety precautions.

By following these steps and adapting to market demands, an equipment rental business can thrive, providing valuable services while generating substantial profits.

CHAPTER FIVE

ROYALTIES

Royalties represent a lucrative avenue for passive income. Whether from books, music, patents, or intellectual property, royalties offer continuous earnings for creators. Once the work is produced, royalties flow in with minimal effort, making it an attractive option for supplementing income streams. While initial investment in creation is required, royalties provide long-term benefits, often lasting years or even generations. With the digital age expanding opportunities, royalties remain a cornerstone of passive income strategies, offering financial stability and the potential for substantial returns without active involvement.

INTELLECTUAL PROPERTY

Intellectual property (IP) represents creations of the mind, such as inventions, literary and artistic works, designs, symbols, names, and images used in commerce. Leveraging intellectual property as a source of passive income involves monetizing rights to these creations, allowing others to use or license them in exchange for royalties or fees.

STARTUP COST

The startup cost for leveraging intellectual property varies depending on the type and scope of the creation. Here are some common examples:

Patents: Obtaining a patent involves filing fees, attorney costs, and potentially expenses for research and development. Prices can range from a few thousand to tens of thousands of dollars, depending on the complexity of the invention and the jurisdictions involved.

Copyrights: Registering a copyright is relatively inexpensive, with fees typically ranging from $35 to $55 per application in the United States. However, costs may increase if legal assistance is required for complex cases.

Trademarks: Registering a trademark involves application fees, which can range from a few hundred to a few thousand dollars, depending on the jurisdiction and the number of classes of goods or services covered.

PROFITABILITY

The profitability of leveraging intellectual property can be substantial, particularly for successful creations with widespread appeal. Consider the following examples:

Patents: According to the United States Patent and Trademark Office (USPTO), the average annual revenue generated by a single patent is estimated to be around $250,000. However, this figure can vary significantly depending on factors such as market demand and the commercialization strategy employed.

Copyrights: Income from copyrighted works can be lucrative, particularly in industries such as publishing, music, film, and software. For example, bestselling authors can earn millions of dollars annually in royalties from book sales and adaptations.

Trademarks: Well-known trademarks can command substantial licensing fees and royalties. For instance, according to Forbes, the licensing revenue generated by the Coca-Cola trademark alone amounted to over $10 billion in 2020.

HOW TO DO IT

Identify Your Intellectual Property: Determine which creations you own or have the rights to, whether they are inventions, artistic works, brand names, or symbols.

Protect Your Intellectual Property: Secure appropriate legal protections, such as patents, copyrights, or trademarks, to safeguard your intellectual property rights and prevent unauthorized use.

Monetize Your Intellectual Property: Explore various avenues for monetizing your intellectual property, such as licensing agreements, royalty arrangements, product sales, or franchise opportunities.

Market Your Intellectual Property: Promote your creations to potential licensees, investors, or buyers through targeted marketing efforts, networking, and participation in industry events.

Monitor and Enforce Your Rights: Stay vigilant against infringement of your intellectual property rights and take prompt action to enforce them through legal means if necessary.

Leveraging intellectual property as a source of passive income offers lucrative opportunities for monetizing creative assets. By understanding the startup costs, profitability potential, and practical steps involved, individuals can capitalize on their intellectual property to generate passive income streams effectively.

MUSIC ROYALTIES

Music royalties represent a lucrative avenue for passive income generation, wherein creators earn royalties from their compositions or performances each time their work is used or performed. This includes royalties from radio play, streaming services, live performances, TV shows, movies, and more. Essentially, by creating original music or investing in existing music rights, individuals can tap into a consistent revenue stream over time.

STARTUP COST:

The startup cost for investing in music royalties can vary widely depending on several factors such as the popularity of the artist, the potential earning capacity of the music, and the platform through which royalties are managed. Prices for purchasing music rights can range from a few hundred dollars to millions, with some high-profile catalogs fetching significant sums in the marketplace. However, platforms like Royalty Exchange or Songtrust offer opportunities for individuals to invest in music royalties with entry-level investments starting from a few hundred dollars.

PROFITABILITY:

The profitability of music royalties can be substantial for successful compositions or catalogs. According to data from the Recording Industry Association of America (RIAA), streaming revenue alone accounted for $11.4 billion in the United States in 2020, representing a 13.4% increase from the previous year. Additionally, performance rights organizations like ASCAP and BMI distribute billions of dollars annually in royalties to songwriters, composers, and publishers worldwide. For instance, top songwriters can earn tens of thousands to millions of dollars annually in royalties from radio play, streaming, and other uses of their music.

HOW TO DO IT:

1. Create Original Music: One approach to earning music royalties is to create and record original music.

Whether you're a singer-songwriter, composer, or musician, recording and releasing your music on digital platforms like Spotify, Apple Music, or YouTube can generate royalties from streams, downloads, and ad revenue.

2. Invest in Existing Catalogs: Another option is to invest in existing music catalogs or rights. Platforms like Royalty Exchange facilitate the buying and selling of music royalties, allowing investors to purchase a share of future royalty earnings from established artists or catalogs. This approach provides a passive income stream without the need for creating music from scratch.

3. Register with Performance Rights Organizations (PROs): Ensure that your music is registered with performance rights organizations such as ASCAP, BMI, or SESAC. These organizations collect royalties on behalf of songwriters, composers, and publishers for performances of their music on radio, TV, live concerts, and other public venues.

4. **Monitor and Manage Royalties**: Stay informed about your royalty earnings by regularly monitoring statements from streaming platforms, PROs, and other sources. Utilize royalty management services like Songtrust to streamline the collection and distribution of royalties from various sources.

In summary, music royalties offer a promising avenue for passive income generation, with the potential for substantial profits over time. Whether by creating original music, investing in existing catalogs, or registering with performance rights organizations, individuals can capitalize on the value of music rights to build a diversified portfolio of passive income streams.

BOOK ROYALTIES

Book royalties represent a passive income stream generated from the sales of published books. Authors receive a percentage of the revenue generated from each sale, providing a consistent source of income over time.

STARTUP COST:

The startup cost for earning book royalties varies depending on factors such as publishing route, editing, cover design, and marketing expenses. Self-publishing platforms like Amazon Kindle Direct Publishing offer a low-cost entry point, with minimal expenses for formatting and publishing. On the other hand, traditional publishing routes may involve higher upfront costs for editing, cover design, and marketing, which can range from a few hundred to several thousand dollars.

PROFITABILITY:

The profitability of earning book royalties can be substantial, albeit variable. According to Author Earnings, self-published authors earn, on average, 60-80% of each book sale, compared to the 10-25% typically received through traditional publishing contracts. For example, a self-published eBook priced at $2.99 with a 70% royalty rate can generate approximately $2.09 in royalties per sale. With effective marketing and a sizable readership, authors can generate significant passive income from ongoing book sales.

HOW TO DO IT:

1. Write Compelling Content: Start by creating high-quality, engaging content that resonates with your target audience. Whether fiction or non-fiction, focus on providing value and meeting reader needs.

2. Choose Your Publishing Route: Decide whether to pursue traditional publishing or self-publishing. Self-publishing offers greater control and higher royalty rates but requires authors to handle aspects such as editing, formatting, and marketing independently.

3. **Prepare Your Manuscript**: Edit and proofread your manuscript thoroughly to ensure it meets professional standards. Consider hiring a professional editor or seeking feedback from beta readers to improve the quality of your work.

4. **Publish Your Book:** If self-publishing, utilize platforms like Amazon Kindle Direct Publishing (KDP), IngramSpark, or Draft2Digital to publish your book in eBook and print formats. Optimize your book's metadata, including title, description, and keywords, to improve visibility and sales potential.

5. Market Your Book: Implement a marketing strategy to promote your book and reach your target audience. Utilize tactics such as social media marketing, email newsletters, book launch events, and collaborations with influencers or bloggers to increase visibility and drive sales.

6. Monitor Sales and Royalties: Regularly monitor your book sales and royalty earnings through your chosen publishing platform's reporting tools. Analyze sales trends, reader feedback, and marketing performance to refine your strategy and maximize profitability over time.

By following these steps and remaining committed to producing quality content and effective marketing, authors can harness the potential of book royalties as a lucrative passive income stream. With persistence and strategic effort, earning passive income from book sales can become a rewarding and sustainable endeavor.

ARTWORK ROYALTIES

Artwork royalties offer artists a unique opportunity to earn passive income from their creations. By licensing their artwork for use in various commercial applications such as merchandise, prints, or digital media, artists can generate ongoing royalties each time their work is sold or utilized.

STARTUP COST:

The startup costs for entering the artwork royalties market can vary depending on factors such as the quality of your artwork, the platforms or agencies you choose to work with, and any associated marketing expenses. Generally, artists may need to invest in high-quality digital or physical prints of their artwork for showcasing and marketing purposes. Prices for these prints can range from a few dollars for digital downloads to hundreds of dollars for premium physical prints or merchandise.

PROFITABILITY:

The profitability of artwork royalties can be significant, especially for artists with a strong portfolio and a loyal fan base. While exact figures may vary, artists typically earn royalties ranging from 5% to 30% of the sale price of each licensed artwork. For example, if a licensed print of your artwork sells for $50, and your royalty rate is 20%, you would earn $10 in royalties for each sale. With multiple artworks licensed across various platforms or merchandise, artists can accumulate substantial passive income over time.

HOW TO DO IT:

1. Create High-Quality Artwork: Begin by creating high-quality artwork that showcases your unique style and creativity. Whether it's digital illustrations, paintings, photographs, or graphic designs, focus on producing compelling pieces that resonate with your target audience.

2. Research Licensing Platforms: Explore online platforms, marketplaces, or licensing agencies that specialize in connecting artists with potential buyers or licensees. Popular platforms such as Redbubble, Society6, or Adobe Stock offer artists the opportunity to upload their artwork and earn royalties from sales or licensing deals.

3. Set Up Licensing Agreements: Once you've chosen your preferred platforms, familiarize yourself with their licensing agreements and submission guidelines. Ensure that you understand the terms of each agreement, including royalty rates, exclusivity clauses, and licensing durations.

4. Promote Your Artwork: Take an active role in promoting your licensed artwork to maximize exposure and sales potential. Utilize social media platforms, artist communities, and your own website or portfolio to showcase your work and attract potential buyers or licensees.

5. Monitor Performance and Royalties: Keep track of your artwork's performance across different platforms and monitor royalty earnings regularly. Adjust your marketing strategies, pricing, or portfolio based on sales trends and feedback to optimize your passive income generation.

In summary, artwork royalties present a lucrative opportunity for artists to monetize their creativity and generate passive income. By creating high-quality artwork, leveraging online platforms, and actively promoting their work, artists can establish a sustainable source of income while showcasing their talent to a wider audience.

CHAPTER SIX

AFFILIATE MARKETING AND REFERRAL PROGRAMS

Affiliate marketing and referral programs offer lucrative avenues for passive income. By promoting products or services through affiliate links, individuals earn commissions for each sale generated. Referral programs extend this concept, rewarding participants for recommending products to others. Both methods capitalize on existing networks and online platforms, requiring minimal ongoing effort once set up. Success hinges on strategic promotion, audience targeting, and cultivating trust. With dedication and savvy marketing tactics, affiliate marketing and referral programs can generate consistent passive income streams, offering financial rewards while leveraging the power of word-of-mouth and online influence.

EARNING COMMISSIONS BY PROMOTING AND SELLING PRODUCTS OR SERVICES THROUGH AFFILIATE LINKS OR REFERRAL PROGRAMS

Affiliate marketing offers a lucrative opportunity to earn commissions by promoting and selling products or services through affiliate links or referral programs. It operates on a simple premise: you recommend products to your audience, and when they make a purchase through your unique affiliate link, you earn a commission. This model eliminates the need for inventory management or customer support, making it an attractive option for aspiring entrepreneurs seeking passive income streams.

STARTUP COST:

One of the most appealing aspects of affiliate marketing is its low barrier to entry. Startup costs typically range from minimal to zero, making it accessible to individuals with varying budget constraints. In fact, you can start affiliate marketing with as little as a website or social media presence, both of which can be established at little to no cost.

PROFITABILITY:

The profitability of affiliate marketing varies depending on factors such as niche selection, audience engagement, and marketing strategies employed. However, successful affiliates can earn significant passive income. According to Statista, the global affiliate marketing spending amounted to $12 billion in 2021, underscoring its immense revenue-generating potential. Commission rates vary across programs but can range from 5% to 50% or even higher in some cases.

HOW TO DO IT:

1. Choose Your Niche: Select a niche that aligns with your interests, expertise, and audience preferences. Focus on niches with high demand and ample affiliate opportunities.

2. Research Affiliate Programs: Explore affiliate networks such as Amazon Associates, ShareASale, or ClickBank to find products or services relevant to your niche. Look for programs with competitive commissions and reliable tracking systems.

3. Create Valuable Content: Produce high-quality content that educates, entertains, or solves problems for your target audience. Incorporate affiliate links naturally within your content, avoiding overly promotional language.

4. *Drive Traffic*: Utilize various marketing channels such as SEO, social media, email marketing, or paid advertising to drive traffic to your affiliate links. Experiment with different strategies to identify what works best for your audience.

5. *Analyze and Optimize*: Monitor your affiliate performance regularly, tracking clicks, conversions, and revenue generated. Optimize your strategies based on data insights to maximize your earnings potential over time.

Examples of Websites Offering Affiliate Services:

1. *Amazon Associates*: The world's largest online retailer offers an extensive affiliate program with millions of products across diverse categories.

2. Commission Junction (CJ Affiliate): A leading affiliate network connecting advertisers with publishers, offering a wide range of affiliate programs from top brands.

3. ShareASale: A user-friendly affiliate network with thousands of merchants and a robust tracking system for affiliate marketers.

Affiliate marketing presents a viable pathway to passive income generation with minimal startup costs and unlimited earning potential. By leveraging affiliate programs, creating valuable content, and driving targeted traffic, individuals can establish profitable affiliate businesses and achieve financial freedom.

CHAPTER SEVEN

DIGITAL PRODUCTS AND ONLINE COURSES

Digital products and online courses offer lucrative opportunities for passive income. By creating valuable content once and leveraging digital platforms, creators can generate continuous revenue streams. Whether it's e-books, software tools, or educational courses, the scalability and accessibility of digital products allow for wide-reaching audiences. Through effective marketing and strategic pricing, creators can monetize their expertise and knowledge. With minimal ongoing effort, these products can generate consistent income, providing financial freedom and flexibility. As the digital landscape continues to expand, tapping into the potential of digital products and online courses remains a promising avenue for passive income generation.

SELLING E-BOOKS, DIGITAL DOWNLOADS, SOFTWARE, OR ONLINE COURSES.

Selling digital products like e-books, software, online courses, and digital downloads offers a lucrative avenue for generating passive income. By leveraging your expertise or creating valuable content, you can reach a global audience and earn recurring revenue long after the initial investment of time and resources.

STARTUP COST:

The startup costs for selling digital products vary depending on factors such as production quality, marketing strategies, and platform fees. Generally, you can start with minimal investment, ranging from as low as $100 for basic equipment and software to a few thousand dollars for professional-grade tools and marketing campaigns.

PROFITABILITY:

The profitability of selling digital products can be substantial, with profit margins often exceeding 70-90% after deducting production and distribution costs. For instance, if you sell an online course priced at $100 with production costs of $20, your profit per sale would be $80. With effective marketing and scalability, digital products have the potential to generate significant passive income. Some successful digital product creators earn six or seven figures annually.

HOW TO DO IT:

1. Choose Your Niche: Identify a niche where you have expertise or a passion for creating content. Conduct market research to validate demand and assess competition.

2. Create High-Quality Content: Develop valuable digital products such as e-books, software, or online courses that address specific pain points or provide solutions to your target audience.

3. Set Up an Online Platform: Choose a platform to host and sell your digital products. Options include self-hosted websites, e-commerce platforms like Shopify or WooCommerce, or specialized platforms like Udemy or Teachable for online courses.

4. Market Your Products: Implement a marketing strategy to drive traffic and sales to your digital products. Utilize content marketing, email marketing, social media promotion, SEO, and affiliate partnerships to reach your audience effectively.

5. *Optimize for Sales:* Continuously analyze and optimize your sales funnel to improve conversion rates and maximize profitability. Monitor customer feedback, tweak pricing strategies, and refine product offerings based on market trends and preferences.

Examples of Websites Offering Affiliate Services:

1. *Amazon Associates:* Amazon's affiliate program allows you to earn commissions by promoting a wide range of products, including e-books, software, and digital downloads available on the platform.

2. *ClickBank:* ClickBank is a popular affiliate marketplace specializing in digital products such as e-books, online courses, and software. It offers a wide selection of products across various niches.

3. *ShareASale*: ShareASale is an affiliate network that features merchants offering digital products, including e-books, software tools, and online courses. It provides a user-friendly platform for finding and promoting relevant products to your audience.

Selling e-books, digital downloads, software, or online courses presents a viable opportunity to generate passive income with relatively low startup costs and high-profit potential. By leveraging your expertise, creating valuable content, and implementing effective marketing strategies, you can build a sustainable passive income stream in the digital products space.

CREATING AND MONETIZING YOUTUBE VIDEOS OR PODCASTS

Creating and monetizing YouTube videos or podcasts is a popular avenue for generating passive income in today's digital landscape. With millions of users consuming content on these platforms daily, there's a vast audience waiting to be tapped into. Whether you're passionate about sharing knowledge, entertaining others, or providing valuable insights, YouTube videos or podcasts offer a versatile platform to showcase your expertise and interests.

STARTUP COST:

The beauty of starting a YouTube channel or podcast is that it can be relatively low-cost, especially compared to traditional business ventures. Essential equipment such as a decent microphone, camera (if creating videos), and editing software can be acquired for as little as $100 to $500, depending on your quality standards and preferences. Additionally, there may be minimal costs associated with hosting platforms or website domains, typically ranging from $10 to $50 per month.

PROFITABILITY:

While success in monetizing YouTube videos or podcasts can vary widely depending on niche, audience size, and content quality, the potential for profitability is significant. According to a study by Influencer Marketing Hub, YouTube creators with over 100,000 subscribers can earn between $12,000 to $25,000 per sponsored video, while top-tier influencers can command upwards of $250,000. Similarly, podcasters can earn substantial revenue through sponsorships, with rates ranging from $18 to $50 per 1,000 listens (CPM). Additionally, affiliate marketing can further boost income, with commissions varying from a few dollars to hundreds per sale.

HOW TO DO IT:

1. Identify Your Niche: Choose a topic or niche that aligns with your interests, expertise, and audience preferences. This could range from lifestyle and personal development to technology and finance.

2. Create Quality Content: Invest time and effort into producing high-quality content that resonates with your target audience. Whether it's educational, entertaining, or informative, compelling content is key to attracting and retaining viewers or listeners.

3. Build Your Audience: Consistently promote your content across social media platforms, engage with your audience through comments and messages, and collaborate with other creators or influencers in your niche to expand your reach.

4. Monetize Your Content: Once you've built a loyal following, explore various monetization options such as advertising, sponsorships, merchandise sales, and affiliate marketing. Websites like Amazon Associates, ShareASale, and ClickBank offer affiliate services across a wide range of industries, allowing you to earn commissions for promoting products or services relevant to your content.

Examples of Websites that Offer Affiliate Services:

1. *Amazon Associates:* With a vast selection of products across virtually every category, Amazon Associates allows creators to earn commissions ranging from 1% to 10% on qualifying purchases made through their affiliate links.

2. *ShareASale*: ShareASale connects creators with thousands of merchants offering diverse products and

services. Affiliates can earn commissions ranging from a few dollars to hundreds per sale, depending on the merchant's payout structure.

3. *ClickBank*: Specializing in digital products such as eBooks, online courses, and software, ClickBank offers affiliates generous commissions, sometimes as high as 75% of the product price. With a wide range of niches and products to choose from, creators can find lucrative opportunities to promote relevant offerings to their audience.

Creating and monetizing YouTube videos or podcasts presents an accessible and potentially lucrative opportunity for individuals to generate passive income. By focusing on quality content creation, audience engagement, and strategic monetization strategies such as affiliate marketing, aspiring creators can build sustainable revenue streams while sharing their passion and expertise with the world.

CHAPTER EIGHT

ADVERTISING INCOME

Advertising income presents a lucrative avenue for passive earnings. By strategically placing ads on websites, blogs, or social media platforms, individuals can generate revenue effortlessly. Leveraging platforms like Google AdSense or affiliate marketing programs, content creators monetize their digital presence, earning income as visitors engage with displayed advertisements. With minimal ongoing effort, this form of passive income offers a scalable opportunity for individuals to capitalize on their online traffic and content, turning their digital footprint into a steady stream of revenue. Through effective audience targeting and content optimization, advertising income becomes a sustainable passive income stream, rewarding creators for their digital efforts.

MONETIZING WEBSITES, BLOGS, OR APPS THROUGH DISPLAY ADS, SPONSORED CONTENT, OR AFFILIATE MARKETING

Monetizing websites, blogs, or apps through display ads, sponsored content, or affiliate marketing offers a lucrative opportunity to generate passive income. By leveraging the traffic and engagement on your digital platforms, you can partner with advertisers or promote affiliate products to earn revenue.

STARTUP COST

The startup cost for monetizing websites, blogs, or apps can vary depending on factors such as platform, hosting fees, and marketing expenses. Generally, the initial investment can range from as low as $100 to $500 for basic setup and promotion. However, this cost can increase as you scale your efforts and invest in premium features or advertising campaigns.

PROFITABILITY

The profitability of monetizing digital platforms depends on factors like niche, audience size, and monetization strategies. According to industry data, websites with high traffic can earn significant revenue through display ads, with average RPMs (revenue per thousand impressions) ranging from $5 to $50 or more, depending on the niche and ad placement.

Similarly, sponsored content can command lucrative fees, with rates varying based on the platform's reach and audience demographics. Affiliate marketing also offers substantial earning potential, with commissions ranging from a few cents to hundreds of dollars per sale, depending on the product or service promoted.

HOW TO DO IT

To monetize your website, blog, or app, follow these steps:

1. Choose a Niche: Select a niche that aligns with your interests and has commercial viability.

2. Build Your Platform: Create a professional website, blog, or app with engaging content and user-friendly design.

3. Drive Traffic: Implement SEO strategies, social media marketing, and content promotion to attract visitors to your platform.

4. Choose Monetization Methods: Decide on the monetization methods that best suit your audience and content, such as display ads, sponsored content, or affiliate marketing.

5. *Partner with Advertisers*: Join ad networks like Google AdSense or affiliate programs relevant to your niche to start earning revenue.

6. *Optimize Performance*: Monitor your analytics, experiment with different monetization strategies, and optimize your content and ad placements for maximum profitability.

Examples of Websites that offer these services

1. *Google AdSense*: Google's advertising platform allows website owners to display targeted ads and earn revenue based on clicks or impressions.

2. *Amazon Associates*: Amazon's affiliate program enables bloggers and website owners to promote products and earn commissions on qualifying purchases made through their referral links.

3. *SponsoredReviews.com*: This platform connects advertisers with bloggers and content creators for sponsored content opportunities, allowing creators to earn money by publishing sponsored posts on their websites or blogs.

In summary, monetizing websites, blogs, or apps through display ads, sponsored content, or affiliate marketing presents a viable pathway to passive income. With strategic planning, quality content, and effective promotion, you can capitalize on your digital presence to generate sustainable revenue streams.

RENTING AD SPACE ON YOUR PROPERTY, CAR, OR OTHER ASSETS.

Renting out ad space on your property, car, or other assets is a creative way to generate passive income. Companies are constantly seeking new avenues to advertise their products or services, and your assets can become valuable real estate for their marketing campaigns.

STARTUP COST:

The startup costs for renting ad space on your assets can vary depending on factors such as location, visibility, and duration of the ad campaign. Generally, the cost ranges from a few hundred to a few thousand dollars. For example, placing advertisements on your car may involve the initial expense of getting a vehicle wrap or magnetic signs, which can range from $500 to $3,000.

PROFITABILITY:

Renting ad space on your assets can be highly profitable, with potential earnings ranging from hundreds to thousands of dollars per month. For instance, a homeowner with a property in a high-traffic area could earn $500 to $1,000 per month by allowing companies to place banners or signage on their fence or lawn. Similarly, a car owner who participates in a vehicle advertising program may earn $100 to $500 per month, depending on the size of the ad and driving habits.

HOW TO DO IT:

1. Identify Your Assets: Determine which assets you own that could be utilized for advertising, such as your property, car, bicycle, or even clothing.

2. Research Advertising Platforms: Explore websites and platforms that connect advertisers with asset owners, such as Carvertise, Wrapify, or Adzze for car advertising, and Airbnb or Rooftop Ads for property advertising.

3. Register and List Your Assets: Sign up on the chosen platform, create a profile, and list your assets available for advertising. Provide details such as location, size, and pricing.

4. Negotiate Terms: Once you receive inquiries from advertisers, negotiate terms such as the duration of the ad campaign, payment structure, and any restrictions or guidelines.

5. Install Ads and Collect Payments: Once the terms are agreed upon, install the advertisements on your assets as per the agreement and collect payments as scheduled.

Examples of Websites:

1. **Carvertise**: Carvertise connects drivers with advertisers who want to reach a wider audience through vehicle advertising campaigns. (Website: carvertise.com)

2. Wrapify: Wrapify offers a platform for drivers to earn passive income by wrapping their cars with advertisements from leading brands. (Website: wrapify.com)

3. **Adzze:** Adzze specializes in unconventional advertising methods, including sticker ads on laptops, coffee cups, and more. (Website: adzze.com)

4. Airbnb: Airbnb allows property owners to rent out ad space on their homes, including banners, signs, or branded experiences, to advertisers looking for unique marketing opportunities. (Website: airbnb.com)

5. Rooftop Ads: Rooftop Ads connects property owners with advertisers interested in utilizing rooftop space for large-scale advertisements visible from a distance. (Website: rooftopads.com)

In summary, renting ad space on your assets presents a lucrative opportunity to earn passive income with relatively low startup costs. By leveraging online platforms and connecting with advertisers, you can monetize your assets and tap into a new revenue stream effortlessly.

CHAPTER NINE

FRANCHISE OWNERSHIP

Franchise ownership offers passive income by leveraging established brands and systems. Owners invest upfront, then earn royalties or a share of profits without active involvement. This model allows for scalability, as multiple franchises can be owned for greater returns. However, success hinges on choosing the right franchise, diligent management, and market conditions. Despite its passive nature, initial investment, ongoing fees, and occasional involvement in strategic decisions are required. Franchise ownership can be a lucrative form of passive income, providing financial stability and potential for growth to savvy entrepreneurs willing to navigate its complexities.

OWNING AND PROFITING FROM FRANCHISED BUSINESSES WHERE YOU RECEIVE A SHARE OF THE PROFITS.

Franchised businesses offer a compelling opportunity to generate passive income by leveraging established brand recognition and proven business models. As a franchisee, you invest in a ready-made system, where you receive a share of the profits in exchange for operating under the franchisor's brand and following their operational guidelines. This arrangement allows you to tap into a lucrative market with reduced risk and a higher chance of success compared to starting a business from scratch.

STARTUP COST

The startup cost for owning and profiting from a franchised business varies widely depending on factors such as industry, brand prestige, and location. Typically, initial investments can range from a few thousand dollars to several hundred thousand dollars. However, this upfront cost covers expenses like franchise fees, equipment, inventory, and initial marketing. Some low-cost franchises can be started for as little as $10,000, while larger, well-known brands may require investments upwards of $1 million.

PROFITABILITY

The profitability of franchised businesses can be substantial, with many offering attractive returns on investment. According to the International Franchise Association (IFA), the average annual revenue for franchise businesses in the United States is around $600,000, with profit margins ranging from 6% to 12%. However, profitability can vary depending on factors such as location, market demand, and the effectiveness of management. Successful franchisees can expect to earn a steady stream of passive income once their business is up and running.

HOW TO DO IT:

To embark on your journey of owning and profiting from franchised businesses, follow these steps:

1. Research: Explore different franchise opportunities to find a business that aligns with your interests, skills, and financial goals.

2. Financing: Determine the startup costs and secure financing through personal savings, loans, or investors.

3. Due Diligence: Thoroughly review the franchise disclosure document (FDD) to understand the terms, fees, and support provided by the franchisor.

4. *Training and Support*: Take advantage of training programs and ongoing support offered by the franchisor to ensure a successful launch and operation.

5. *Marketing and Operations:* Implement marketing strategies to attract customers and follow operational guidelines to maintain consistency and quality.

6. *Monitor and Adjust:* Continuously monitor your business performance, solicit feedback from customers, and make necessary adjustments to optimize profitability.

Examples of Websites Offering Franchise Opportunities:

1. *Franchise Direct (www.franchisedirect.com):* A comprehensive platform featuring a wide range of franchise opportunities across various industries and investment levels.

2. Franchise Gator (www.franchisegator.com): An online directory offering a curated selection of franchise opportunities with detailed information on startup costs, requirements, and support provided.

3.Entrepreneur Franchise 500 (www.entrepreneur.com/franchise500): An annual ranking of the top franchise opportunities worldwide, providing valuable insights into industry trends and emerging brands.

In summary, owning and profiting from franchised businesses can be a lucrative avenue for generating passive income. By carefully selecting the right franchise, managing operations effectively, and leveraging the support of the franchisor, you can build a successful business venture that yields consistent returns over time.

CHAPTER TEN

NETWORK MARKETING OR MULTI-LEVEL MARKETING (MLM)

Network Marketing, also known as Multi-Level Marketing (MLM), offers a pathway to passive income by leveraging social networks and team building. Participants earn commissions not only from their sales but also from the sales of their recruits and their recruits' recruits, forming a hierarchical structure. Advocates tout its potential for flexibility and scalability, allowing individuals to generate income beyond their direct efforts. However, critics highlight its resemblance to pyramid schemes and the potential for exploitation. Success in MLM often requires significant time and effort upfront, with passive income emerging over time through sustained team growth and product sales.

EARNING PASSIVE INCOME THROUGH COMMISSIONS FROM SALES MADE BY YOUR DOWNLINE OR NETWORK.

Earning passive income through commissions from sales made by your downline or network is a concept rooted in multi-level marketing (MLM) or affiliate marketing models. Essentially, you leverage your network to promote and sell products or services, earning a percentage of the sales made by those you've recruited into your downline.

STARTUP COST:

The startup cost for this venture can vary widely depending on the specific MLM or affiliate program you choose to join. Typically, startup costs range from as low as $50 to several hundred dollars. Some programs may require the purchase of a starter kit or product inventory, while others have minimal entry fees.

PROFITABILITY:

The profitability of earning passive income through commissions can be significant for those who build large and active networks. Commissions are usually calculated as a percentage of the sales generated by your downline, ranging from 5% to 30% or more. For example, if your downline generates $10,000 in sales in a month, and your commission rate is 10%, you would earn $1,000 in passive income.

HOW TO DO IT:

1. Research: Explore different MLM or affiliate programs to find one that aligns with your interests, values, and financial goals.

2. Join: Sign up for the program and familiarize yourself with its products or services, compensation plan, and marketing tools.

3. Build Your Network: Recruit others to join your downline and provide them with training and support to help them succeed.

4. Promote: Utilize various marketing channels such as social media, email marketing, and content creation to promote the products or services to your network and beyond.

5. Track and Optimize: Monitor your sales performance, track your commissions, and continually optimize your marketing strategies to maximize your passive income potential.

Examples of Websites:

1. Amway: Amway is one of the oldest and most well-known MLM companies, offering a wide range of health, beauty, and home care products.

2. Avon: Avon operates on a direct selling model, allowing representatives to earn commissions on their sales as well as the sales of their downline.

3. Amazon Associates: Amazon Associates is an affiliate marketing program that enables individuals to earn commissions by promoting Amazon products on their websites, blogs, or social media platforms.

Earning passive income through commissions from sales made by your downline or network can be a lucrative opportunity with the potential for significant returns. However, success in this venture requires dedication, perseverance, and effective marketing strategies to build

and nurture a thriving network.

CHAPTER ELEVEN

STORAGE INCOME

Storage income offers a lucrative avenue for passive earnings. By renting out unused space, such as garages, attics, or storage units, individuals can generate a steady stream of income without active involvement. Platforms like Airbnb, Neighbor, or StoreAtMyHouse facilitate this process, connecting renters with those in need of storage. With minimal effort and investment, individuals can capitalize on the growing demand for storage solutions. This passive income stream not only provides financial stability but also maximizes the utility of underutilized spaces, offering a win-win scenario for both owners and renters.

RENTING OUT STORAGE SPACE, SUCH AS SELF-STORAGE UNITS OR GARAGE SPACE.

Renting out storage space, whether it's self-storage units or unused garage space, is a lucrative passive income opportunity. With the increasing demand for storage solutions due to urbanization and the rise of online businesses, there's a growing market for individuals seeking affordable and accessible storage options.

STARTUP COST:

The startup cost for renting out storage space can vary depending on the scale of the operation and location. Setting up a self-storage facility may require significant capital investment for land acquisition, construction, and security systems, with costs ranging from tens to hundreds of thousands of dollars. On the other hand, renting out garage space involves minimal startup costs, primarily consisting of minor renovations or security enhancements, typically ranging from a few hundred to a couple of thousand dollars.

PROFITABILITY:

The profitability of renting out storage space can be substantial. Self-storage facilities boast high-profit margins, with an average annual return on investment ranging from 8% to 12%. For example, a small self-storage facility with 100 units rented at an average rate of $100 per month could generate monthly revenue of $10,000, resulting in annual revenue of $120,000 to $144,000.

Renting out garage space can also be profitable, with potential monthly earnings ranging from $50 to $300 per space, depending on factors such as location, size, and amenities. With minimal overhead costs, garage rentals can yield impressive returns on investment, providing a steady stream of passive income.

HOW TO DO IT:

1. Assess Your Space: Determine whether you have suitable storage space available, such as an empty garage or unused rooms.

2. Prepare the Space: Clean, organize, and make any necessary improvements to ensure the space is secure and suitable for storage.

3. Set Competitive Rates: Research local market rates for storage space and set competitive rental prices to attract tenants.

4. Advertise Your Space: Utilize online platforms and classified ads to market your storage space to potential renters.

5. *Screen Tenants:* Screen prospective tenants to ensure they are reliable and trustworthy.

6. *Create Rental Agreements:* Draft comprehensive rental agreements outlining terms and conditions, payment schedules, and security deposit requirements.

7. *Provide Secure Access:* Implement security measures such as locks, surveillance cameras, and access control systems to protect the stored belongings.

8. *Manage Rental Payments:* Establish a system for collecting rental payments promptly and efficiently.

Examples of Websites Offering These Services:

1. *SpareFoot:* A platform that allows individuals to list and rent out self-storage units online.

2. *Neighbor:* A peer-to-peer marketplace for renting out unused space, including garages, basements, and attics.

3. Stashbee: An online platform connecting individuals in need of storage space with hosts offering spare rooms, garages, and other storage solutions.

In summary, renting out storage space presents a practical and profitable passive income opportunity. Whether you choose to invest in self-storage facilities or rent out unused garage space, careful planning, strategic pricing, and effective marketing can help you maximize your earnings and build a successful passive income stream.

CHAPTER TWELVE

AUTOMATED BUSINESSES

Automated businesses offer a lucrative avenue for passive income. Leveraging technology, these enterprises operate with minimal human intervention, reducing overhead costs and maximizing efficiency. From dropshipping e-commerce stores to automated software solutions, opportunities abound. Once set up, they generate income continuously, requiring little ongoing effort. This passive income stream offers financial freedom and flexibility, allowing entrepreneurs to focus on other pursuits while their automated systems handle operations seamlessly. With the right strategies and execution, automated businesses can serve as reliable sources of income, providing a pathway to financial stability and independence.

DEVELOPING AUTOMATED ONLINE BUSINESSES, SUCH AS DROPSHIPPING, PRINT-ON-DEMAND, OR SOFTWARE AS A SERVICE (SAAS) MODELS.

Automated online businesses, such as dropshipping, print-on-demand, or Software as a Service (SaaS) models, represent innovative ways to generate passive income in today's digital landscape. These business models leverage technology to streamline operations, minimize overhead costs, and maximize profitability, making them attractive options for aspiring entrepreneurs.

STARTUP COST: The startup costs for these automated online businesses can vary depending on the chosen model and individual preferences. Here's a general overview:

1. Dropshipping: Typically, the startup costs for dropshipping are relatively low, ranging from $500 to $2,000. This includes expenses for setting up a website, purchasing a domain, marketing, and initial inventory procurement.

2. Print-on-Demand: Startup costs for print-on-demand businesses are also relatively modest, ranging from $500 to $1,500. This includes expenses for website development, design software subscriptions, product samples, and marketing.

3. SaaS (Software as a Service): Startup costs for SaaS businesses can be higher due to development and infrastructure expenses. They typically range from

$5,000 to $50,000 or more, depending on the complexity of the software and the scale of operations.

PROFITABILITY:

The profitability of automated online businesses can vary based on factors such as niche selection, marketing strategy, and operational efficiency. However, these models have the potential to generate significant passive income over time. Here are some approximate figures:

1. Dropshipping: Dropshipping businesses can achieve profit margins ranging from 10% to 30%, depending on product selection and pricing strategies. With effective marketing and scaling, it's possible to generate monthly profits ranging from $1,000 to $10,000 or more.

2. Print-on-Demand: Profit margins for print-on-demand businesses typically range from 30% to 50%. With a strong marketing presence and quality designs, monthly profits can range from $500 to $5,000 or higher.

3. SaaS (Software as a Service): SaaS businesses often have high-profit margins, ranging from 60% to 90% or more. Monthly profits can vary widely based on subscription pricing and customer acquisition, but successful SaaS startups can generate tens of thousands of dollars or more in recurring revenue.

HOW TO DO IT:

To start an automated online business, follow these general steps:

1. Choose Your Niche: Select a niche with high demand and low competition, ensuring there's a viable market for your products or services.

2. Set Up Your Website: Use platforms like Shopify, WooCommerce, or Squarespace to create your online store or SaaS platform. Customize it to reflect your brand and offerings.

3. Source Products/Develop Software: For dropshipping and print-on-demand, find reliable suppliers or manufacturers. For SaaS, develop or outsource the development of your software solution.

4. Market Your Business: Implement digital marketing strategies such as social media advertising, SEO, email marketing, and content marketing to attract customers and drive sales.

5. Optimize and Scale: Continuously monitor and optimize your business processes, website performance, and marketing campaigns to maximize profitability. As your business grows, scale up operations and explore expansion opportunities.

Examples of Websites:

1. Dropshipping: Shopify (www.shopify.com), Oberlo (www.oberlo.com)

2. Print-on-Demand: Printful (www.printful.com), Teespring (www.teespring.com)

3. SaaS: HubSpot (www.hubspot.com), Slack (www.slack.com)

By following these steps and leveraging the resources available through platforms like Shopify, Printful, and HubSpot, aspiring entrepreneurs can embark on their journey to building automated online businesses and creating passive income streams.

CHAPTER THIRTEEN

FINANCIAL PRODUCTS

Financial products offer avenues for passive income, generating earnings with minimal effort. Dividend-paying stocks provide regular payouts, while bonds offer fixed interest payments. Real estate investments yield rental income, requiring limited involvement once established. Exchange-traded funds (ETFs) track market indexes, offering diverse investment opportunities without active management. Peer-to-peer lending platforms allow investors to earn interest on loans to individuals or businesses. Additionally, high-yield savings accounts and certificates of deposit (CDs) provide stable returns with little risk. Harnessing these financial instruments intelligently can build a steady stream of passive income, enhancing financial stability and future prospects.

HIGH-YIELD SAVINGS ACCOUNTS, CERTIFICATES OF DEPOSIT (CDS), OR MONEY MARKET ACCOUNTS.

High-yield savings accounts, certificates of deposit (CDs), and money market accounts are popular low-risk investment options for individuals seeking to generate passive income. These financial instruments offer competitive interest rates, making them attractive alternatives to traditional savings accounts.

STARTUP COST:

The startup cost for investing in high-yield savings accounts, CDs, or money market accounts varies depending on the financial institution and the minimum deposit requirements. Generally, opening these accounts can be relatively affordable, with minimum deposit thresholds ranging from as low as $100 to $1,000 or more.

PROFITABILITY:

The profitability of high-yield savings accounts, CDs, and money market accounts lies in the interest earned on deposited funds. While interest rates fluctuate over time, these accounts typically offer higher yields compared to standard savings accounts. For instance, as of [current date], the average APY (Annual Percentage Yield) for high-yield savings accounts ranges from 0.50% to 0.80%, CDs offer rates varying from 0.50% for short-term CDs to over 1.50% for longer-term CDs, and money market accounts provide yields averaging around 0.40% to 0.60%.

HOW TO DO IT:

1. *Research Financial Institutions:* Begin by researching reputable banks or credit unions that offer high-yield savings accounts, CDs, or money market accounts.

2. *Compare Interest Rates and Terms:* Compare the interest rates, minimum deposit requirements, and terms offered by different financial institutions to find the best option suited to your financial goals and risk tolerance.

3. *Open an Account:* Once you've identified a suitable account, follow the institution's procedures to open the account and deposit funds.

4. *Monitor and Reinvest:* Monitor your account regularly to track interest earnings and consider reinvesting dividends or interest payments to maximize your passive income potential.

Examples of Websites Offering These Services:

1. Ally Bank (www.ally.com): Ally Bank offers high-yield savings accounts with competitive interest rates and no monthly maintenance fees. They also provide a range of CD options with varying terms and yields.

2. Marcus by Goldman Sachs (www.marcus.com): Marcus offers high-yield online savings accounts and CDs with attractive rates and no fees. Their user-friendly platform makes it easy to manage your investments.

3. Discover Bank (www.discover.com): Discover Bank provides high-yield savings accounts, CDs, and money market accounts with competitive rates and flexible terms. They offer 24/7 customer support and convenient online banking services.

In summary, high-yield savings accounts, CDs, and money market accounts offer accessible and low-risk opportunities for generating passive income. By conducting thorough research, comparing options, and leveraging reputable financial institutions, individuals can harness the potential of these investment vehicles to grow their wealth steadily over time.

ANNUITIES OR STRUCTURED SETTLEMENTS

Annuities and structured settlements are financial instruments designed to provide a steady stream of income over a specified period, often used as a form of passive income. Annuities involve purchasing an insurance product that pays out regular payments, while structured settlements are typically awarded as part of a legal settlement and paid out over time.

STARTUP COST

The startup costs for investing in annuities or structured settlements can vary depending on factors such as the amount invested and the specific terms of the agreement. Generally, purchasing an annuity requires a lump sum payment or a series of payments over time. Annuities can range in price from a few thousand dollars to several hundred thousand dollars, depending on the desired payout and length of the contract.

PROFITABILITY

The profitability of annuities or structured settlements depends on various factors, including the interest rates, payout terms, and length of the investment. While annuities offer a guaranteed stream of income, the returns may be lower compared to other investment options. Structured settlements, on the other hand, are often tax-free and can provide a reliable source of income for those receiving them.

For example, a $100,000 fixed annuity with a 5% annual interest rate could provide approximately $416 per month in income. Similarly, a structured settlement worth $250,000 paid out over 20 years could yield roughly $1,041 per month, depending on the terms of the agreement.

HOW TO DO IT

Investing in annuities or structured settlements typically involves working with financial advisors or insurance companies that specialize in these products. It's essential to research and compare different options to find the best fit for your financial goals and risk tolerance.

Here are some websites that offer information and services related to annuities and structured settlements:

1. Annuity.org: This website provides comprehensive resources and tools for understanding and purchasing annuities, including calculators and educational articles.

2. Structuredsettlements.com: As a leading provider of structured settlement services, this website offers information on selling structured settlement payments, as well as resources for those receiving structured settlements.

3. Investopedia.com: While not specific to annuities or structured settlements, Investopedia offers in-depth articles and guides on various financial topics, including annuities, that can help you make informed decisions.

While annuities and structured settlements can offer a reliable source of passive income, it's essential to carefully consider the terms, risks, and potential returns before investing. By researching your options and consulting with financial professionals, you can make informed decisions that align with your long-term financial goals.

CHAPTER FOURTEEN

CRYPTOCURRENCY AND BLOCKCHAIN

Cryptocurrency and blockchain offer avenues for passive income through various means such as staking, lending, and yield farming. Staking involves holding cryptocurrencies in a wallet to support the network and earn rewards. Lending platforms enable users to lend their crypto assets for interest. Yield farming allows investors to earn rewards by providing liquidity to decentralized finance (DeFi) protocols. These methods offer passive income streams, albeit with varying degrees of risk. Investors should conduct thorough research and understand the volatility and potential risks associated with the crypto market before engaging in passive income strategies.

STAKING CRYPTOCURRENCIES TO EARN REWARDS

Staking cryptocurrencies involves participating in the validation process of a blockchain network by locking up a certain amount of coins to support its operations. In return, participants receive rewards, similar to earning interest on traditional savings accounts. This process helps secure the network and incentivizes holders to contribute to its functionality while earning passive income.

STARTUP COST:

The startup cost for staking cryptocurrencies varies depending on the coin and the platform used. Generally, users need to hold a minimum amount of the cryptocurrency to participate in staking. This can range from as low as $100 for some coins to several thousand dollars for others. However, with the rise of staking pools and services, users can often join without needing to meet the full requirement individually.

PROFITABILITY:

The profitability of staking cryptocurrencies can be attractive, especially compared to traditional savings accounts. Annual returns typically range from 5% to 20%, depending on the coin and market conditions. For example, staking popular coins like Ethereum or Cardano can yield annual returns of around 5% to 7%, while newer or more volatile coins may offer higher returns, reaching up to 20% or more.

HOW TO DO IT:

1. Choose a Staking Coin: Research and select a cryptocurrency that offers staking rewards and aligns with your investment goals.

2. Set Up a Wallet: Download and set up a compatible wallet that supports staking for your chosen cryptocurrency.

3. Acquire the Cryptocurrency: Purchase the required amount of the cryptocurrency you wish to stake from a reliable exchange.

4. Stake Your Coins: Transfer the coins to your staking wallet and follow the instructions provided by the platform to start staking.

5. Monitor and Reinvest Rewards: Keep track of your staking rewards and consider reinvesting them to compound your earnings over time.

Examples of Websites:

1. Binance: One of the largest cryptocurrency exchanges, Binance offers staking services for various coins, including Ethereum 2.0, Cardano, and Polkadot.

2. Kraken: Another reputable exchange, Kraken provides staking options for popular crypto-currencies like Tezos, Cosmos, and Algorand.

3. Coinbase: A user-friendly platform, Coinbase offers staking services for select crypto-currencies, such as Ethereum and Algorand, through its Coinbase Wallet.

4. StakeFish: A dedicated staking platform, StakeFish supports multiple coins and provides staking pools for users to join and earn rewards collectively.

In summary, staking crypto-currencies presents an opportunity to earn passive income by supporting blockchain networks and contributing to their security and functionality. With relatively low startup costs and the potential for attractive returns, staking has become an appealing option for investors seeking to diversify their passive income streams in the rapidly evolving world of cryptocurrency.

YIELD FARMING AND LIQUIDITY PROVIDING IN DECENTRALIZED FINANCE (DEFI) PLATFORMS.

Yield farming and liquidity providing are innovative strategies within the realm of decentralized finance (DeFi) that allow individuals to earn passive income by contributing assets to liquidity pools. In DeFi platforms, users provide liquidity for various cryptocurrency pairs, and in return, they receive rewards such as interest, fees, or governance tokens.

STARTUP COST:

The startup cost for yield farming and liquidity providing can vary based on the platform and the specific cryptocurrency pair chosen. Generally, it ranges from a few hundred to several thousand dollars, depending on the liquidity pool's size and the chosen DeFi protocol. It's crucial to carefully assess and manage risks before committing funds.

PROFITABILITY:

The profitability of yield farming and liquidity providing in DeFi platforms can be attractive. Annual Percentage Yields (APY) often range from 10% to well over 100%, depending on market conditions, demand for the provided liquidity, and the chosen platform. It's essential to note that higher returns typically come with increased risk, and market fluctuations can impact profitability.

Example: On the popular DeFi platform Uniswap, liquidity providers earn a share of the trading fees proportional to their share in the liquidity pool. As of [current date], the average APY for some liquidity pools on Uniswap ranges from 20% to 50%.

HOW TO DO IT:

1. **Choose a DeFi Platform**: Select a reputable DeFi platform such as Uniswap, SushiSwap, or PancakeSwap.

2. **Select Cryptocurrency Pairs**: Decide which cryptocurrency pairs you want to provide liquidity for. Typically, stablecoin pairs are less volatile and offer more stable returns.

3. **Acquire Assets**: Obtain the cryptocurrencies you plan to contribute to the liquidity pool.

4. **Provide Liquidity**: Deposit your assets into the chosen liquidity pool. In return, you'll receive liquidity pool tokens representing your share.

5. **Stake Liquidity Pool Tokens:** Some platforms require users to stake their liquidity pool tokens to earn

additional rewards, such as governance tokens or additional fees.

Example Platforms:

1. [Uniswap](https://uniswap.org/): A leading decentralized exchange protocol.

2. [SushiSwap](https://sushi.com/): Known for its community-driven approach and innovative features.

3. [PancakeSwap](https://pancakeswap.finance/): A decentralized exchange on the Binance Smart Chain with lower transaction fees.

Remember, thorough research and due diligence are crucial before venturing into yield farming and liquidity providing. Stay informed about market conditions, platform security, and potential risks associated with different DeFi protocols.

CHAPTER FIFTEEN

REAL ESTATE CROWD-FUNDING

Real Estate Crowdfunding offers a passive income avenue where investors pool funds to collectively invest in real estate projects. It democratizes access to real estate investments, requiring minimal effort from participants. Through online platforms, individuals can invest in various properties, ranging from residential to commercial, without the burdens of property management. Returns come from rental income and property appreciation. While it provides passive income potential, investors should conduct thorough research, assess risks, and consider diversification. Real Estate Crowdfunding offers a convenient way to participate in the real estate market without the hassles of direct ownership, making it an attractive option for passive income seekers.

INVESTING IN REAL ESTATE PROJECTS THROUGH CROWD-FUNDING PLATFORMS, TYPICALLY WITH LOWER CAPITAL REQUIREMENTS COMPARED TO TRADITIONAL REAL ESTATE INVESTMENTS.

Investing in real estate projects through crowd-funding platforms offers individuals an opportunity to participate in property ventures with lower capital requirements compared to traditional real estate investments. These platforms pool funds from multiple investors to finance real estate projects, providing access to a diverse range of properties and investment opportunities.

STARTUP COST:

The startup cost for investing in real estate through crowd-funding platforms typically ranges from as low as

$500 to $10,000, depending on the platform and the specific project. This low barrier to entry allows individuals to begin investing in real estate with smaller amounts of capital compared to purchasing properties outright.

PROFITABILITY:

The profitability of investing in real estate through crowd-funding platforms can vary depending on the specific project and market conditions. However, investors can potentially earn attractive returns, with average annual returns ranging from 8% to 12%, according to industry data. These returns can include rental income, capital appreciation, and dividends from real estate investment trusts (REITs).

HOW TO DO IT:

1. Research Platforms: Start by researching and comparing different crowd-funding platforms that specialize in real estate investments. Look for platforms with a track record of successful projects, transparent fees, and a user-friendly interface.

2. Due Diligence: Conduct thorough due diligence on the available investment opportunities. Review project details, financial projections, and the track record of the project sponsor or developer. Evaluate factors such as location, market demand, and potential risks.

3. Investment: Once you've selected a suitable project, sign up on the crowd-funding platform and complete the investment process. Most platforms allow investors to contribute funds online and track their investments through a dashboard.

4. Monitor Performance: Keep track of your investments and monitor the performance of the underlying real estate projects. Stay informed about any updates or developments provided by the platform or project sponsor.

Examples of Websites:

1. Fundrise: Fundrise is a popular crowd-funding platform that offers investment opportunities in real estate projects across the United States. Investors can choose from a range of investment options, including eREITs and real estate development projects, with a minimum investment starting at $500.

2. RealtyMogul: RealtyMogul allows investors to invest in a variety of real estate assets, including commercial properties, multifamily housing, and debt investments. The platform offers both individual property investments and diversified investment funds, with minimum investments starting at $1,000.

3. *CrowdStreet:* CrowdStreet connects accredited investors with institutional-quality real estate investments, such as commercial properties and multifamily developments. Investors can browse and invest in projects with minimum investment amounts typically ranging from $10,000 to $25,000.

In summary, investing in real estate projects through crowd-funding platforms provides an accessible and potentially lucrative avenue for individuals to diversify their investment portfolios and generate passive income with lower capital requirements compared to traditional real estate investments.

CHAPTER SIXTEEN

UTILITY AND PATENT INCOME

Utility and patent income can serve as lucrative passive streams. Utility patents grant exclusive rights to inventors, allowing them to profit from their innovations. This income can flow steadily as long as the patent remains valid and in demand. With proper management, patent portfolios can generate substantial royalties from licensing agreements or outright sales. Leveraging intellectual property in this way can provide consistent returns without active involvement, making it an attractive option for entrepreneurs and innovators seeking to diversify their income streams.

EARNING INCOME FROM UTILITY PATENTS, WHICH GRANT EXCLUSIVE RIGHTS TO INVENTORS OF A NEW PROCESS OR MACHINE.

Earning income from utility patents presents a lucrative opportunity for inventors who have devised a new process or machine. Utility patents grant exclusive rights to the inventor for a set period, typically 20 years, allowing them to monetize their innovation through licensing agreements, royalties, or outright sales.

STARTUP COST:

The startup cost for obtaining a utility patent can vary widely depending on factors such as complexity, legal fees, and geographic location. On average, filing a utility patent application can range from $5,000 to $15,000, including attorney fees and government filing fees.

However, this investment can yield substantial returns over time.

PROFITABILITY:

The profitability of earning income from utility patents can be significant, with potential returns far exceeding the initial investment. For example, consider the case of a patented invention generating royalties. With a typical royalty rate of 3% to 5%, an invention generating $100,000 in annual revenue could result in $3,000 to $5,000 in passive income per year.

HOW TO DO IT:

1. Conduct thorough research: Before pursuing a utility patent, conduct comprehensive research to ensure that your invention is novel and non-obvious. This may involve searching existing patents, scientific literature, and market trends to assess the viability of your idea.

*2. **Work with a patent attorney***: Engage a qualified patent attorney or agent to help navigate the complex process of obtaining a utility patent. They can provide valuable expertise in drafting and prosecuting your patent application, increasing the likelihood of success.

*3. **Explore licensing opportunities***: Once your patent is granted, explore licensing opportunities with companies operating in relevant industries. Licensing agreements allow you to grant others the right to use your patented invention in exchange for royalties or upfront fees.

*4. **Monitor and enforce your rights***: Continuously monitor the market to ensure that others are not infringing on your patent rights. If infringement occurs, take appropriate legal action to enforce your rights and protect your investment.

Examples of Websites:

- *LegalZoom* (www.legalzoom.com): LegalZoom offers patent filing services, including utility patents, with transparent pricing and access to experienced patent attorneys.

- *UpCounsel* (www.upcounsel.com): UpCounsel connects inventors with patent attorneys specializing in utility patents, offering personalized legal assistance at competitive rates.

- *Google Patents* (patents.google.com): Google Patents provides a free, searchable database of patents worldwide, allowing inventors to conduct prior art searches and assess the patent landscape before filing.

Earning income from utility patents offers inventors the opportunity to capitalize on their innovations and generate passive income streams. By understanding the startup costs, profitability potential, and steps involved, aspiring inventors can navigate the patenting process with confidence and unlock the financial rewards of their creativity.

LICENSING PATENTS TO COMPANIES FOR USE IN THEIR PRODUCTS OR SERVICES.

Licensing patents to companies for use in their products or services is a lucrative avenue for generating passive income. As a patent holder, you possess exclusive rights to your invention, and by licensing it, you grant others the permission to utilize your technology in exchange for royalties.

STARTUP COST

The startup cost for licensing patents varies depending on factors such as the complexity of the invention and the industry. However, prices typically range from a few hundred to several thousand dollars for initial patent filing and maintenance fees. Additionally, legal fees may be incurred for drafting and negotiating licensing agreements.

PROFITABILITY

Licensing patents can be highly profitable, with potential royalties ranging from 1% to 10% or more of the licensee's sales revenue. For instance, if a company generates $1 million in sales from a product incorporating your patented technology and you negotiate a 5% royalty rate, you could earn $50,000 annually in passive income.

HOW TO DO IT

1. Secure Your Patent: Begin by filing a patent application with the appropriate intellectual property office to protect your invention.

2. Identify Potential Licensees: Research companies operating within your invention's industry and identify potential licensees who could benefit from integrating your technology into their products or services.

3. Negotiate Licensing Agreements: Reach out to potential licensees to discuss licensing opportunities. Negotiate terms such as royalty rates, payment schedules, and exclusivity provisions.

4. Draft Contracts: Work with a qualified attorney experienced in intellectual property law to draft licensing agreements that clearly outline the rights and obligations of both parties.

5. *Monitor Compliance:* Monitor licensee activity to ensure compliance with the terms of the licensing agreement and track royalty payments.

Examples of Websites

1. Innoget (innoget.com): Innoget is an open innovation platform that connects inventors with companies seeking innovative technologies for licensing opportunities.

2. Patexia (patexia.com): Patexia is a patent marketplace that facilitates patent transactions, including licensing deals, between patent holders and potential licensees.

3. Yet2 (yet2.com): Yet2 is a technology transfer platform that connects innovators with companies interested in licensing patented technologies for commercialization.

Licensing patents for use in products or services offers a compelling pathway to passive income generation. By protecting your invention, identifying potential licensees, negotiating favorable licensing agreements, and leveraging online platforms, you can transform your intellectual property into a valuable revenue stream.

CHAPTER SEVENTEEN

LICENSING AND FRANCHISE AGREEMENTS

Licensing and franchise agreements offer lucrative avenues for passive income. In licensing, intellectual property rights like patents, trademarks, or copyrights are leased to others for a fee, granting them the right to use the property without transferring ownership. Franchising involves granting individuals the right to operate under an established brand, with ongoing support and guidance, in exchange for fees and royalties. Both models allow for minimal involvement while generating steady revenue streams. However, careful legal and contractual considerations are crucial to protect interests and ensure compliance. Ultimately, these arrangements empower entrepreneurs to leverage existing assets for sustained financial gain with relatively low active involvement.

LICENSING YOUR BRAND, TECHNOLOGY, OR BUSINESS MODEL TO OTHERS IN EXCHANGE FOR ROYALTIES OR FEES.

Licensing your brand, technology, or business model involves granting permission to others to use your intellectual property in exchange for royalties or fees. This can include trademarks, patents, copyrights, or even your unique business processes. Essentially, you're allowing others to leverage your assets to generate revenue while you collect passive income.

STARTUP COST

The startup cost for licensing your brand, technology, or business model can vary widely depending on factors such as the value of your intellectual property and the terms of the licensing agreement. Costs may include legal fees for drafting contracts, marketing expenses to attract potential licensees, and any necessary modifications or updates to your intellectual property. Prices can range from a few hundred to several thousand dollars, but the potential return on investment can be substantial.

PROFITABILITY

The profitability of licensing your intellectual property can be significant. Royalty rates typically range from 3% to 10% of the licensee's sales, but they can vary based on industry standards and negotiation terms. For example, if your brand generates $100,000 in licensed sales at a 5% royalty rate, you would earn $5,000 in passive income. With multiple licensees or high-demand intellectual property, the earnings can quickly add up.

HOW TO DO IT

To begin licensing your brand, technology, or business model, start by identifying the unique aspects of your intellectual property that have value to others. Conduct market research to assess demand and potential competitors. Then, consult with a legal expert to draft a licensing agreement that outlines the terms, duration, and compensation structure. Next, market your licensing opportunities through online platforms, industry events, or direct outreach to potential licensees. Finally, negotiate terms with interested parties and monitor compliance to ensure ongoing revenue generation.

EXAMPLES OF WEBSITES

Several websites offer services to facilitate licensing agreements between intellectual property owners and potential licensees:

1. InventRight: This platform specializes in helping inventors and entrepreneurs license their patents and inventions to companies seeking innovative products.

2. Franchise Direct: While primarily focused on franchising, Franchise Direct also provides resources for licensing business models to interested parties.

3. Brand Licensing Europe: This annual trade show and online platform connect brand owners with licensees across various industries, including fashion, entertainment, and consumer goods.

By leveraging these resources, you can streamline the process of licensing your intellectual property and maximize your passive income potential.

PURCHASING FRANCHISE RIGHTS TO OPERATE A BUSINESS UNDER AN ESTABLISHED BRAND.

Investing in franchise rights to operate a business under an established brand is a popular avenue for generating passive income. Franchising offers the opportunity to leverage the reputation and proven business model of a well-known brand, reducing the risk associated with starting a new venture from scratch. By purchasing franchise rights, individuals gain access to comprehensive support, including training, marketing assistance, and ongoing guidance, to help ensure the success of their business.

STARTUP COST:

The startup cost for purchasing franchise rights can vary widely depending on factors such as the industry, brand recognition, and location. Franchise fees typically range from thousands to hundreds of thousands of dollars, with additional expenses for equipment, inventory, and initial operating costs. While the initial investment can be significant, it provides access to an established customer base and the potential for high returns.

PROFITABILITY:

Franchising offers the potential for lucrative returns on investment. According to the International Franchise Association, franchise businesses generate over $800 billion in annual revenue in the United States alone. Profitability varies by industry and individual franchise location, but successful franchise owners can achieve substantial profits. For example, a popular fast-food franchise may generate annual revenues exceeding $1 million, with net profits ranging from 10% to 20%.

HOW TO DO IT:

*1. **Research***: Start by researching different franchise opportunities to find a brand that aligns with your interests, skills, and financial goals. Consider factors such as brand reputation, demand for products or services, and franchise support offerings.

*2. **Financial Planning***: Assess your financial resources and determine the startup costs associated with purchasing franchise rights. Secure financing if necessary, either through personal savings, loans, or investors.

*3. **Franchise Disclosure Document (FDD)***: Review the franchise disclosure document (FDD) provided by the franchisor, which contains essential information about the franchise system, including costs, obligations, and restrictions.

4. Legal Assistance: Seek legal advice from a franchise attorney familiar with franchise laws and regulations. They can help review the franchise agreement, negotiate terms, and ensure you understand your rights and obligations as a franchisee.

5. Training and Support: Take advantage of the training and support provided by the franchisor to learn the ins and outs of operating the business successfully. Utilize marketing materials, operational guidance, and ongoing assistance to maximize your chances of success.

Examples of Websites:

1. Franchise Direct (www.franchisedirect.com): A comprehensive online directory of franchise opportunities across various industries, offering detailed information and resources for aspiring franchisees.

2. *Franchise* *Opportunities* *Network* (www.franchiseopportunities.com): A platform that connects entrepreneurs with franchise opportunities, providing access to a wide range of brands and investment levels.

3. *Franchise* *Gator* (www.franchisegator.com): A leading franchise directory featuring thousands of franchise opportunities, along with articles, guides, and tools to help individuals explore and research franchising options.

Investing in franchise rights can be a lucrative way to generate passive income while benefiting from the support and recognition of an established brand. With careful research, financial planning, and dedication, individuals can build a successful business and achieve their financial goals through franchising.

. . . .

Special note to the reader:

Andrew Mark
Wishes you success on your passive income journey!